# WHERE THERE'S SMOKE, THERE'S

### A Surefire *Manly* Guide to Ribs and Rubs and Smokin' Good Grub

# BARBECUE!

## BY QUINN L. ORR

Design copyrighted 2014 by Covenant Communications, Inc.
American Fork, Utah

Copyright 2014 by Quinn Orr
Photography © Spencer Burnside, Megan Burnside and
Quinn Orr 2014
Cover and book design by Mark Sorenson © 2014
Covenant Communications, Inc.

Printed in China
First Printing: April 2014

20 19 18 17 16 15 14     10 9 8 7 6 5 4 3 2 1

ISBN-13: 978-1-62108-695-6

# TABLE OF CONTENTS

## About the Author

Quinn "Sparky" Orr was raised on a pig farm on the rolling plains of Southern Alberta; he loves to cook and never gets tired of pork. When he was a child, his mother had an open kitchen policy: if you're hungry, go cook yourself something to eat. When he became a Boy Scout, he spent a lot of time practicing how to cook things over an open fire in the backyard. As a teenager he built his first barbecue by welding together some discarded blades from road graders. The first thing he cooked was steak and beans, and his father said it was the best he had ever eaten.

As an adult, his work as an Emmy Award–winning film producer/director has allowed him to sample and study the cooking techniques of many cultures in more than thirty countries around the world, including a two-year stop in France and Belgium. He loves to create good food and loves to teach others how to do it too. Quinn lives with his wife, family, and four barbecues in Farmington, Utah.

## Acknowledgments

Special thanks are due to my partner Jack Prince and his wife, Janet, for their undying optimism and for journeying with us in the delicious world of barbecue. Also to the food staging and photo team—Christian Orr and Megan and Spencer Burnside—for giving up their Saturdays so generously. Also thanks to Carmen Toth for ideas and feedback. Above all, thanks to my lovely bride, Susan, who makes everything better.

# INTRODUCTION
# "LOVE IS SMOKIN' HERE"

This is a little book that takes on a big subject. If you want to learn the true art of classic barbecue—the art of smoky ribs, pulled pork, chicken, and brisket—but aren't sure where to start, this book is for you. There are a variety of barbecue philosophies out there, and a lot of really big books have been written on how to cook barbecue—but I say start small and simple. One day you may want to get one of those big books, but in the meantime this book will teach you the basics. Once you've got those down pat, you can decide where to go from there.

When I finally accepted the reality that there was a higher way of cooking, I became a student of "life according to barbecue"! One of the first things I learned is that barbecue is many things to many people. To your wife, it's a welcome offer to cook dinner. For your family and friends, it's a social event that includes comfort food. And for you, it's a chance to eat some of the best-tasting meat on the planet while receiving gratitude and compliments from all. In short, it's a celebration of life.

I once went to a survival presentation by a former Navy Seal (if there is such a thing as a *former* Navy Seal). During the presentation he kept returning to one overriding principle. He said that he loved equipment—loved having lots of the gizmos and gadgets that hikers and survivalists love—but they weren't the most important things. As great as equipment is, he said, skills trump equipment: if you have the skills, you don't need much equipment because you know how to do without. But, he insisted, while skills are great, there is something that trumps skills: community. When you are part of a unified group, the very diversity of their knowledge, skills, and resources will always trump an individual trying to make it on his or her own.

Barbecue is like that. You may watch those mobile pit masters and wish you had their 100-foot Huxley Wonder Overdrive Double-Ought Riot Smoker—but the reality is, you don't need that if you have the skills. This book will teach you those skills. Once

# Grilling Is Not Barbecue!

The first thing we need to establish is the difference between grilling and barbecuing. American culture often uses the two words interchangeably, but there *is* a difference.

*Grilling* involves quickly cooking meat or vegetables directly over a hot fire and moving them around to keep them from burning until they're cooked. *Barbecue,* on the other hand, involves slowly cooking meat or vegetables over long periods of time over an indirect heat source and in the presence of smoke. The slow-cooking makes the meat tender, and the smoke provides the signature flavor of true barbecue.

While there is a lot of gray area between grilling and barbecuing, there are foundational techniques and recipes associated with traditional barbecue. You'll get those in this book.

you have the skills, you can invite people over to your house, and they will have to be seriously messed up if they turn down barbecue. That's all there is to it: You will start building your own community! Once you have your own community, you will never have to ask for directions again, because if you've ever hung out with a bunch of guys eating barbecue, you know they'll give you their opinion on everything, even if you don't ask!

I have spent years studying the philosophies and secrets of barbecue, and now I share my humble knowledge and skills with you. That's not all: You'll get some of my opinions on life, even though you didn't ask. I hope you enjoy it.

# The History of Barbecue: Making the Best of a Bad Situation

Barbecue is arguably the most popular form of North American cuisine our culture has produced. Its roots find themselves in the Southern states, with specific barbecue styles cropping up in Kansas, Mississippi, Texas, and the Carolinas. While the methods and flavors vary, all barbecue originates from the same need: trying to cook a lousy cut of meat so that it tastes good. The Holy Grail of barbecue is pork ribs, but let's face it—who in their right mind would choose a cut that was mostly bones with small amounts of meat between them?

In those days, if you could afford it, you chose the tender cuts: the steak or the tenderloin—anything but the ribs. Those who couldn't afford the "good meat" took the ribs. But just because they were limited financially didn't mean they were limited creatively. They discovered marinades and slow-cooking to make the ribs tender, spices to enhance the flavor, and barbecue sauces to make an otherwise undesirable cut simply irresistible. Making the best of a bad situation is what has given us one of the most significant contributions to the American cuisine landscape!

As men, we can expect that sometime during our lives we're going to get the short end of the stick. Chaos happens, and nobody gets a free pass. Everyone is going to encounter something that just isn't fair, and he's going to have to deal with it. You see it in popular culture: Men are the new minority that is being ridiculed and criticized. Just watch a few movies or a few episodes of any TV series—you'll see

that the mom is always smarter than the dad, the kids are smarter than the mom, and the dog is smarter than the kids. But we don't have to buy in to that role! It's important to have a sense of yourself and a perspective of the world around you. You can't always choose the situations in your life, but you can choose how you react to them. Be happy today with what you have today. Work hard to learn skills and build your own community. And if the world gives you a bad cut, start the fire and make barbecue!

# The Fire and Spice Full Sighs Intermountain Barbecue Team

Years ago my buddy Jack and I became students of barbecue. We both loved barbecue and wanted to master the art. When I talked him into buying a smoker cabinet, The Fire and Spice Full Sighs Intermountain Barbecue Team was born.

Our goal was to compete in the Kansas City–sanctioned events and win. We studied recipes and came up with our own. We studied the methods of the past winners and became disciples of their ways. We cooked every chance we could get—Fourth of July, family reunions, business parties, and church gatherings. Our family and friends consistently told us, "This is the best barbecue we have ever had!" We finally felt we were ready to compete head-to-head.

As spring rolled around, we looked at the competition schedule. There were a lot of events. We looked at the investment in time and money. It was high. We both had jobs that required a lot of focus and families we didn't want to abandon. We finally realized that while winning would be nice, at this point in our lives we preferred being the Number-One Barbecue Champions of our families and friends, and we decided to keep it that way—at least for now.

Someday we may compete. We're keeping a few recipes secret just in case—but until then, we want to give our friends and family the wonderful experience of great hometown barbecue.

I have since considered the choice to put my competition dream aside, and don't regret it. I realize that at this point in my life, just because I *can* do something doesn't mean I *should*. For every yes I put out there, a no might have to be given down the road. My good friend Chance Thomas passed on some advice he got from his

mother: "If you go through life always expecting to be number one, most of the time you will be disappointed; but if you go through life expecting to be among the best, you can have a great life."

As the Fire and Spice team, we are happy being among the best—and according to all the people we feed, that is exactly what we are. Feel free to join us!

# GETTING STARTED

If you are going to compete under current Kansas City BBQ competition rules, you have to cook on charcoal. But if your arena is your backyard and you just want to have a great time barbecuing, cook on whatever works for you and don't worry about someone else's rules. While there *are* a few things that make it a lot easier to enter the world of true barbecue, there are far more exceptions and variations out there than there are hard-and-fast rules. Like life, you will ultimately have to experiment a little and decide for yourself what works best for you. With that in mind, let's get down to basics.

First of all, it's important to understand the difference between grilling and barbecuing. *Grilling* may be what you've done so far—you put a piece of meat directly over fire and a few minutes later, you feed it to your family. I enjoy grilling, and it has its place, but it's not barbecue. *Barbecue* is taking pieces of meat that you have pre-seasoned and cooking them slowly at low temperatures to make them tender as they soak up aromatic smokes that add flavor.

There is a place for both grilling and barbecuing in your life, but don't confuse one with the other. One is a skill; the other is an art.

# The Grill

There are a lot of different grills and barbecue cookers out there—some very expensive, others not so much. Chances are you already have one. Since barbecue is about cooking at low temperatures, I think the most important thing to look for is a unit with enough grill space that you can turn on a burner in one section but have plenty of room in the other section to cook meat with indirect heat.

The grill should also have a cover that keeps the smoke in. I have a well-used Weber propane grill with a built-in smoker box and water tray. I love the control of the gas and the efficiency of the smoke box. I have also used a Weber "flying saucer" charcoal grill, a Smoky Mountain smoker cabinet, a Black Diamond drop box charcoal grill, and a couple of other units whose names I don't remember. Each cooker has its own personality—and just like choosing a girlfriend or a

wife, you have to look around and spend a little time with her until you decide, "This is the one for me!" If you already have a grill, keep it until you have tried some of the techniques; then you can determine for sure if a change is in order (and please don't apply this part of the analogy to your wife!).

Eventually, you might want to get into the upper end of barbecue equipment, like a Traeger wood pellet smoker, a Kamado-style ceramic egg smoker, or a Texas-style dedicated trailer. But let's start simple for now.

Assuming you have a grill, let's talk about what comes next. Simply, it's the three primary factors that make barbecuing different from grilling: smoke, temperature, and rubs. Of those three, smoke comes first.

# Smoke

Several different types of wood are used in traditional American barbecue, but none is better known than hickory. It is the Grand Dame of smoke flavors and a great place to start. I prefer hickory; if I'm going to the effort of cooking barbecue, I want that classic flavor. But it's completely a personal choice.

Other popular woods are mesquite, apple, and cherry—and there are a host of others. My barbecue partner, Jack, prefers cherry for everything he does. It works well with all cuts and doesn't overpower more subtle foods, such as chicken and salmon.

Many places that sell charcoal or other barbecue supplies also sell wood chips. For a couple of bucks at Wal-Mart, you can get a bag of wood chips and start creating those great flavors.

Smoke is created by exposing the wood to heat that would normally make it burst

# Everything Tastes Better with Smoke

One evening, I brought an uncooked pizza home and decided to cook it on the grill. I fired up the grill, added some hickory chips, and put the pizza on a pizza stone atop the rib rack. Everyone raved about it and said it was the best pizza they had ever had. It was just the regular take-and-bake I always buy, but the smoke made it very exotic.

into flame—but you either limit the oxygen that can get to the wood chips or you soak them in water before using them. As a result, the combustion process is incomplete, and you get smoke. The chips can be added directly to your fire if you are already cooking with wood or charcoal, in which case they should be soaked in water beforehand (follow the directions on the bag). Another way is to purchase a smoker box from a home and garden store. But one of the easiest ways to start smoking on any grill is by making a smoker packet.

To make a smoker packet, wrap a few cups of wood chips in an envelope of aluminum foil, then pierce the top a number of times with a pen or pencil to create holes for the smoke to escape. When you start cooking, place the packet directly over the hot side of your grill, either on the grill or on the baffles over your burner if you have them. Depending on what you are cooking, you may need to make several packets during the

cooking process to get the amount of smoke you want. As an experiment, make up a packet and throw it on your grill next time you make burgers and dogs. Put the meat on after the packet starts to smoke, lower the temperature a little, keep the lid down, and taste the difference a good smoke can make.

# Recipes Are For Wimps!

Recipes are for wimps. Here's why: most people who write recipes want you to follow them exactly, as if the slightest deviation would result in the downfall of civilization as we know it. The reality is that the ingredients you use will vary much more than recipe writers are willing to admit.

There are lots of practical illustrations of this. I remember when I first used reliable old Heinz ketchup in England. It tasted completely different there! I think they used cider vinegar rather than white vinegar, and they added a stronger clove flavor; it was decidedly different from what I was used to. The flavor of meats will also change from place to place; for example, the barley-fed beef of western Canada tastes much different than the corn-fed beef of the United States. Here's the bottom line: if you're going to cook barbecue and own the art, you will have to look at a recipe and learn the *principle* of how the ingredients work together. Once you are able to do that, you will make adjustments based on the flavor of the ingredients available in your area and suited to your own tastes.

Don't get me wrong—I'm giving you some recipes that you may really like and never want to change, but chances are you will want to tweak them a little. That's why I recommend that you get a small, hardback notebook and write on the front page "Secret Family Recipes." When you try a recipe, write it down. After you're done, make notes about what you liked or disliked. If it's too salty or sweet or not spicy enough, write it down. The next time you cook, modify the recipe based on your notes. Continue the process until it's perfect for your ingredients and conditions.

Recipes are like advice; we often seek it from friends and family, but we never really intend to follow it exactly. No one situation is exactly the same as another, and we seldom do exactly what we're told. That wouldn't make sense *or* be manly! We all have to find our own way. Keeping a journal will let you find your own combinations that work for your particular set of circumstances and those for whom you cook. The recipes in this book are not definitive; they are a starting point. The path you choose from there is up to you.

# Temperature

The next thing you need for serious barbecuing is two thermometers—one on your grill and a second one to monitor the internal temperature of the meat. Barbecuing is like being in any relationship: Appearances can be deceiving, and you need to know what's going on under the surface. Barbecue is about low temperatures and slow cooking time, but it's all engineered so that the right things are happening on the inside, because that's what's most important.

For some cuts to become tender, they must be held at a certain internal temperature for a certain period of time. If the temperature is too high, the outside will burn or dry into jerky; if the temperature is too low, the meat will never get tender—or, even worse, you may face the health risks of eating uncooked meat! Thermometers are like road trips with your significant other: When you ask, "How are you doing?" she lets you know what's going on under the surface so you can adjust as you go and not get burned.

As mentioned, the first thermometer you need is for monitoring the temperature in the grill. A lot of grills have thermometers built into their covers. If yours doesn't, you can buy one in the home and garden section of many stores and mount it onto the cover by drilling just one hole. Some of the very large, wood-fired, trailer-mounted grills have several thermometers at different locations, because temperatures will vary three-dimensionally over almost any cooking surface. Over time, you will learn how to take advantage of that variation to cook thicker pieces faster and thinner pieces slower so they are all done at the same time.

The second thermometer is for monitoring the temperature at the core of the meat you are cooking. Meat thermometers come in all shapes and sizes, from a traditional circle-face

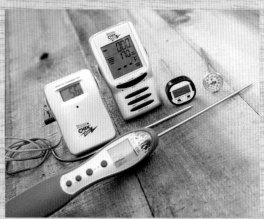

# Temperature and Time

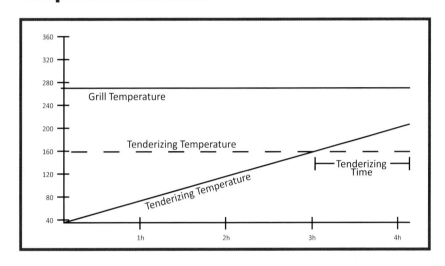
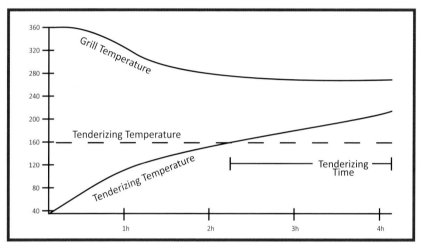

The classic cuts of barbecue, by their very nature, are tough. It is through slow-cooking that they achieve their wonderful flavor and texture, but only if the right temperature is achieved. Meat starts to cook and give up its natural juices at 140 degrees Fahrenheit, but the parts of the meat that cause toughness don't start to melt until 160 degrees Fahrenheit. At this point the oils replace the lost liquids and create a tender cut. The amount of tenderness depends on how long the internal temperature cooks at 160 degrees or higher, which is why it makes sense to start your cooking process hotter to "jump start" the internal rise of temperature and facilitate a longer cooking time at the effective levels. If the internal temperature is not high enough, the meat will still be tough despite the slow cook.

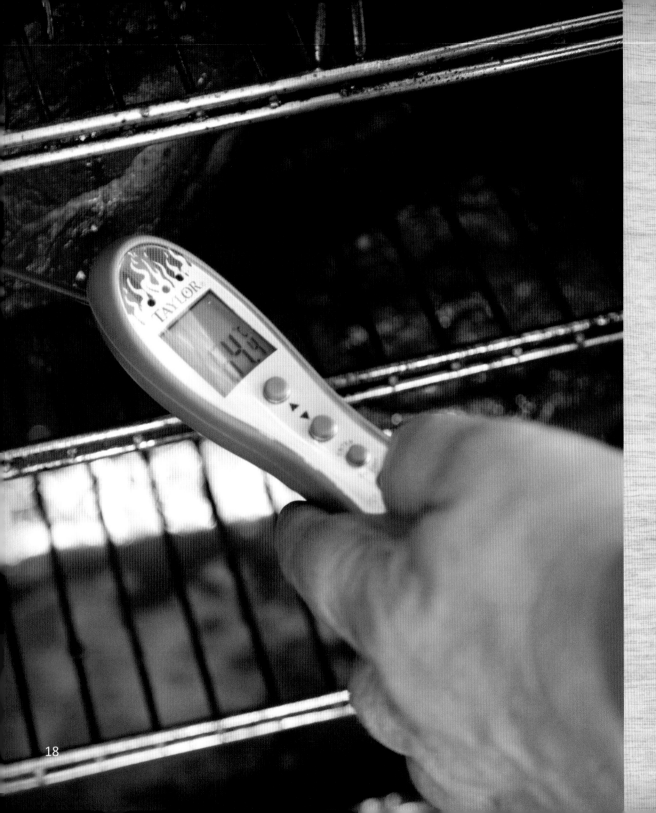

analog type to an instant-read digital or a radio-sending unit that broadcasts the temperatures to a receiver you keep in your pocket. (Ask for that one for Father's Day! I've been given two now, and I love them!) I have used all the different kinds of meat thermometers and they all work, but my favorite is the instant-read, as it reduces the amount of time you spend with your hand in the fire.

The guidelines for taking temperatures are rather straightforward: push the probe into the meat as far as you can without touching bone; bone conducts heat, so a thermometer that is touching bone gives a false reading. Once the meat hits a certain internal temperature, the FDA considers the meat safe to eat—but that definitely does *not* mean it is "done." Once you hit the recommended internal target temperature, the tenderness of the meat depends on how long you can keep the meat at that temperature. In other words, the length of time you keep the meat at a particular temperature will determine how tender it becomes.

Barbecuing is a balancing act between internal and external temperatures. If you cook at a temperature that is too high, the outside will be burned by the time the inside is cooked. If you cook at a temperature that is too low, the outside may look great, but the inside could be raw.

The relationship between external and internal temperatures looks something like this: Start cooking at a high temperature with the grill rather hot, in order to get the internal temperature to rise quickly. Starting this way also helps the rub seal the meat. After the internal temperature is rising nicely, drop the external temperature so as not to burn the exterior, and hold it there. We like about 350 degrees to start; then after a time, depending on the thickness of the cut, drop the temperature to somewhere between 215 and 275. Starting too low may result in the meat coming to temperature toward the end of the cooking period, but the meat will probably not be tender because it wasn't at the desired temperature long enough.

The required temperatures vary depending on the type of meat you are cooking. For example, beef prime rib is considered "rare" at the relatively low 140 degrees F.; the temperature is higher if you want medium or well-done meat. Brisket, however, has to be brought to temperature and held there in order to become tender. Pork and poultry are considered to be done at 170 to 180 degrees F.

Great barbecuing consists of heating the cut quickly at the beginning to seal the meat and get the interior temperature rising then lowering the temperature to keep the exterior pretty while the interior cooks slowly. Of the two, interior temperature is the most important. There are other things you can do to preserve outward appearances. One of them is the type of rub you use.

## Minimum Safe Cooking Temperatures

| | |
|---|---|
| **BEEF** | 145 |
| **POULTRY** | 165 |
| **PORK** | 145 |
| **HAM** | 140 |
| **GROUND MEATS** | 160 |
| **CASSEROLES** | 165 |

(Courtesy of www.foodsafety.gov)

## Drying Brown Sugar

Dark brown sugar brings a nice flavor to rubs but must be dried before you use it in a rub. To make your own, sprinkle a bag of brown sugar through a sieve onto a baking sheet to make a layer ¼ to ½ inch deep. Place in the oven on the middle rack at 250 degrees F. After a couple of hours, it will be a dry cake that needs to be broken up. Run it through a sieve or mesh colander and store in a zip-lock bag to keep out humidity. You'll have enough for several batches of rub.

## Rubs

A *rub* is a combination of spices and other ingredients designed to add flavor to your meat. I have never found a commercial rub I like and have always created my own. The rubs I have developed are formulated for great flavor but also to seal in moisture.

When using rubs, you will soon develop the ability to know how much to use. Large cuts of meat (like a pork shoulder for pulled pork) have a relatively small surface area per pound of meat and can take a lot more rub than cuts that have a large surface area for the amount of meat (like ribs).

I build my rubs from a common base and then add other ingredients to create the final flavor I want. This takes some experimentation, but you'll pick it up after a few tries. Don't get nervous—spices are strangely forgiving, and I have never had an experiment make my meat inedible, even if it wasn't exactly what I was shooting for.

# FIRE AND SPICE WHITE RUB

1 C. salt

1 C. sugar

½ C. onion powder

½ C. garlic powder

¼ C. custom flavoring (optional)

Mix all ingredients in a bowl. Store in an empty spice container with a shaker lid.

Fire and Spice White Rub is great when you want to enhance the flavor of mild meats without overwhelming them with heavy spices (like those found in the Fire and Spice Red Rub). I use this rub on chicken, fish, and pork. It is generally not strong enough for beef. This recipe makes about three cups, which will get you through a couple of cookouts without remixing. If you wish to make more or less, use the ratios to make a bigger or smaller batch.

You can use this rub plain, which I often do; for variation, try adding a few tablespoons of dried thyme, oregano, rosemary, or Italian seasoning. The amount will vary depending on the freshness of the herbs. Fresh herbs tend to be stronger in flavor, in which case you would want to use less. This will give your chicken and fish an herbal Italian/Mediterranean flavor.

You can also replace the regular salt with kosher or pretzel salt; these salts have a flake-like consistency, don't dissolve as easily, and tend to be perceived as "saltier." If you use one of these salts, you may want to use less in the rub. One cup is generally the most salt I would ever use in the rub, as taste preferences in my part of the West tend to lean toward sweet rather than salty.

You can also vary your rub by adding other custom flavorings, such as celery seed, orange zest, lime zest, dry mustard, wasabi powder, or most of the "green" herbal spices.

# "More" Is Part of the Barbecue Recipe

As you learn the art of barbecue, you will notice that you use large quantities of ingredients. While some cooks use a shake of salt or a dash of pepper on their food, barbecue calls for cups of salt, chili powder, and paprika; handfuls of herbs; and entire bottles of barbecue sauce. That's part of what makes barbecue what it is: a complex mix of flavor and texture. Perhaps that is why it appeals to the male psyche. Men tend to like things that are bigger, faster, and stronger. Successful barbecue wouldn't be what it is without the "more" of spices and sauces, balanced according to the preference of the cook. When you start trying these recipes, I suggest you go to the dollar store, a restaurant supply store, or some other place where you can buy spices in bulk. You will use a lot of these spices, and there is no sense in spending "more" than you have to.

If you are interested in a stronger, spicier mix, try the Fire and Spice Red Rub recipe.

# FIRE AND SPICE RED RUB

1 C. dried brown sugar

½ C. white sugar

½ C. paprika

½ C. salt

½ C. chili powder

¼ C. onion powder

¼ C. garlic powder

1 tsp. black pepper

½ tsp. ground red pepper

Mix all ingredients in a bowl. Store in an empty spice container with a shaker lid.

Variations on this recipe can include different ratios of brown and white sugar or other unrefined sugars. You can also introduce a smoky flavor by using smoked paprika, smoked black pepper, or smoked black salt. The mild chili pepper can be replaced by a New Mexico chili pepper mix—but if you do use a chili pepper mix, you may want to leave out the black and red peppers, as it's pretty spicy already. The black and red peppers can also be replaced with powdered ancho, habañero, wasabi powder, or other exotic hot peppers. Try it, taste it, and modify to your preferences—then write it down, and you have a secret family recipe! It's your rub—make it your own!

As you refine your recipes, pay attention to the ratios of hot pepper, salt, and sugar that you use. These are the main flavors that can make or break your rub. In the Intermountain West, where we do most of our cooking, people tend to like their barbecue sweeter and not too salty or spicy. In other parts of the country, those preferences change. As you gain more confidence in mixing spices, your recipe will change until you find just the right combination to delight the people for whom you cook. As mentioned before, keep your salt and spice lower for cuts with a lot of surface, like ribs, and crank it up for those with low surface area, such as pulled pork roasts.

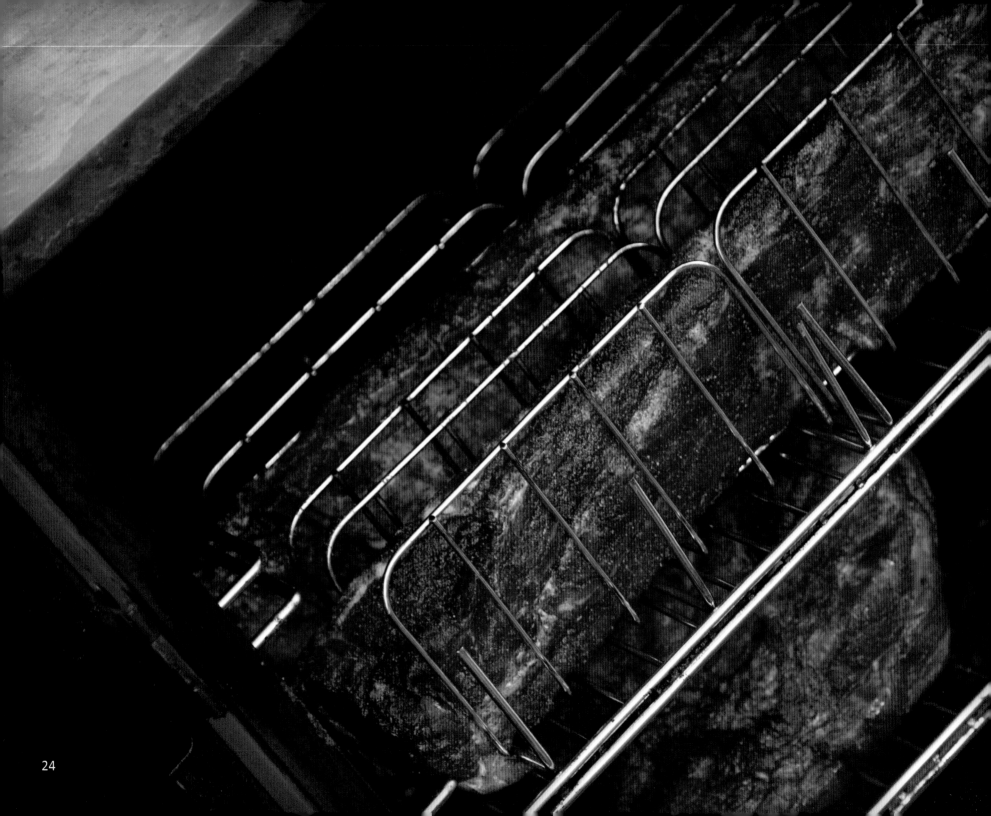

# COOKING THE BASIC CUTS OF BARBECUE

Now that you have the basics, it's time to start cooking. While any cut of meat can be barbecued, there is a traditional set of cuts that is considered the mainstay of barbecue: pork ribs, pulled pork, beef brisket, and chicken. (There is no cut specified for chicken—the bird is the "cut," so choose whatever part you want.) Depending on where you live, there are other great cuts traditionally added to barbecue menus, such as sausage, tri-tip, and prime rib. The list and variations are almost endless, so we're going to focus on the basics; you can branch out after you've mastered them.

The following "Barbecue Missions" are sequenced in order of difficulty. You may want to start using the simple techniques and work your way up. Or you might want to jump right in at the top. Remember, it's up to you.

# Mission 1-Barbecued Chicken Thighs

For a regular backyard griller, chicken is a difficult challenge: the skin never crisps evenly; the meat is often dry; and by the time the inside is cooked, the outside is burned. For the student of barbecue, however, this is what you'll cook when you want to do something easy!

## PREPARATION

First of all, don't use chicken breasts; they're too hard to keep moist, and they require more advanced techniques that you'll learn later. Start with a package of chicken thighs: they are more flavorful, and when cooked correctly, most people can't tell if they're white meat or not—and, frankly, they won't care because the chicken tastes so good!

Sometimes I buy skinless, boneless thighs; other times I use the regular bone-in, skin-on variety. The important thing to remember is to not cook them with the skin on. To remove chicken skin, use a kitchen towel to grab a corner of the skin and rip it off. I generally leave the bone in, but it doesn't make that much difference if you want to cut it out. If you are serving several types of meat, you might want to cut each thigh in two so people can take smaller pieces. Trim off any large pieces of fat then sprinkle the pieces of chicken completely with white rub—use more rub than you would salt, but not so much that it cakes. Lay the pieces of chicken on a baking sheet side by side; leave enough space

# Barbecue Sauces

There are a lot of barbecue sauces out there, with flavors focusing on smoke, brown sugar, honey, and fruity flavors, such as raspberry, chipotle, and mango. In many circles, cooks prefer to create their own from scratch, while others simply use commercial brands. As a student of barbecue, you will want to try different varieties and find the flavors that are most appealing to you and those for whom you cook. One way to do this is to find two or three sauces that you like and mix them together to create a new flavor. If anyone asks you how you made it, you can say it's a secret family recipe—and you won't even be stretching the truth.

Another method is to create variations of the commercial sauces you like by adding a spoonful of garlic, onion, ground red pepper, vinegar, molasses, or even orange zest, according to your own taste preferences. There are many possibilities!

If you do want to try making barbecue sauce from scratch, here's a recipe I like:

24 oz. ketchup

½ C. brown sugar

¼ C. molasses

¼ C. Worcestershire sauce

¼ C. vinegar

2 T. yellow mustard

1 T. garlic powder

1 T. onion powder

Combine ingredients in a saucepan; simmer slowly 10–12 minutes, or until thick. If the sauce is too thin, stir 2 T. cornstarch into the mix when it's cold; it will thicken faster when it is time to caramelize it.

between them so the rub doesn't get brushed off. Once the meat has been rubbed, it can be refrigerated on trays for up to twenty-four hours, during which time the rub will work its way into the meat. The timing is completely optional; I usually rub just a few minutes before cooking.

## COOKING

Heat the grill to 350 degrees F, banking the charcoal to one side (or using only one burner if you are using a gas grill). Put a smoker packet, box, or soaked wood chunks directly over the fire; place the chicken on the unheated section of the grill. Hold the temperature at 350 for 10–15 minutes. This will be long enough to let the ingredients bond together and create the protective sealing coat that keeps the meat tasty and moist. Although thighs are small and can be cooked at higher temperatures or over direct heat, for this technique adjust the grill to drop the temperature to 225 after the initial

scald. This will allow the meat to be exposed to more smoke while it cooks, letting it acquire a richer flavor.

Keep the cover of the grill down as much as possible to keep the smoke and heat in. The smoker packet should generate a continuous flow of smoke for about 15 minutes. If it runs out and you want more, put on a new wood chip packet, but don't open the hood too often, as it lets the heat and smoke escape.

Most grills have sections that run hotter or cooler than others; start by putting the thicker pieces in the hotter areas, then rotating them as they cook until all are done. The meat is done once the internal temperature reaches 180 degrees, but it can be held on the grill longer if you wish to continue smoking or glazing.

I like the Kansas City–style of barbecue, where the sauce is added during cooking. Some prefer to serve it on the side or

# Caramelizing Barbecue Sauces

Caramelizing sauce on the grill is a little tricky. If you want a great look and also want to save time, put all the meat on a tray, cover it with sauce, and put it under the broiler of the oven on a middle rack. Watch it carefully. After a minute or two, the sauce will start to bubble and thicken. When it comes to a rolling boil, take it out of the oven. Or, if you want to live dangerously, wait until the edges of the sauce turn brown or black. (This is a method that cannot be used during competition, because cooks are required to use nothing but charcoal.)

not add it all. (For details on which sauce to use, see the sidebar, "Barbecue Sauces.") I generally squeeze the sauce directly from the bottle onto the meat and then smooth it with a brush. I do that for two reasons: first, the grill is hot, and it's faster than dipping and brushing; second, you can spread it on thicker, which is always a good thing in my book. The sauce needs to be caramelized until it is thick, like icing on a cake. This usually takes about 10–15 minutes on the grill, or even less time if you use my secret method and put it under the broiler. (See the sidebar, "Caramelizing Barbecue Sauces.") You might consider coating the bottom of the meat first, then turning and glazing the top so both sides are covered and it looks nice when you present it.

# Mission 2-Pulled Pork

Pulled pork is a large cut of pork roast that is slow-cooked until it is tender enough to be pulled into shreds; it is served plain or mixed with barbecue sauce and is eaten in a sandwich or as an entrée. Pulled pork is one of the longest cooks you can do on a grill; it cooks from 8 to 32 hours, depending on the size of the roast.

In order to do such a long cook, you will need some additional tools—a spray bottle

or a small mop for thin liquids that are actually called "mops" themselves. The purpose of the mop is to keep the outside of the meat from turning into jerky while it is cooking over a long period of time. For starters, use something simple and effective: apple juice. For other recipes, see the "Mops" section in the "Other Barbecue Techniques" chapter.

## PREPARATION

Choose a pork roast, such as a partial pork shoulder or a Boston butt. Cut and trim

any extra fat back to ¼–½ inch. Some people estimate about one pound of raw meat per person you are planning to feed, but I generally find that ½–¾ pound is plenty if you have a good variety of side dishes. Sprinkle the meat liberally with Fire and Spice Red Rub and work the rub into cracks and crevices. Use plenty of rub—pulled pork can take the thickest rub of any of the barbecue cuts.

## COOKING

Preheat the grill to 350 degrees and place the roast on the unheated side of the grill, fat side up, directly on the grill. Add a smoker packet to the hot side of the grill. Keep the grill at 350 degrees for about 15 minutes, allowing the searing and sealing of the meat, and then drop the temperature to about 225. Use a spray bottle to spray the roast every 20–30 minutes with the apple juice to keep the exterior moist. Replace the smoker packets as necessary. Since you have a lot of meat and will be cooking it for

# Gloves

The art of barbecue requires the serious student to get his hands dirty, so to speak. When you barbecue, you handle raw cuts of meat, rub exotic spice mixtures into roasts, cut hot sauce–glazed ribs, and pull steaming pork roasts into shreds. These processes can be irritating to the skin—but that irritation can be easily avoided by using sterile disposable gloves to protect your hands. I personally like the blue Nitrile style that I get at the local pharmacy, but there are several different types you can try. Gloves protect your hands from the juices, spices, heat, and fat of barbecuing and let you work much faster.

One word of caution: *Do not recycle the gloves*. Discard any gloves you use on raw foods before you handle any cooked products.

a long time, you might go through more than one bag of chips to get the flavor you want.

Under normal conditions, the outside of the roast will get very dark brown or even black but will not have a charred flavor. If it does, you can cut the dark portion off and discard it during the shredding process. Generally, it is not necessary to move or turn pork roasts while cooking at these low temperatures. Leaving the roast in one position will also allow the fat cap on the meat a chance to melt and work its way through the cut to add flavor and moisture.

Cook the roast about 1½–2 hours per pound. Boston butts and similar roasts take 12–24 hours to cook. A whole pork shoulder can take 24–32 hours, so you might want to start with a smaller cut.

The important issue is to watch the internal temperatures to gauge doneness. The temperature must come up to 185–195 degrees to be sufficiently hot to melt the fat marbling in the meat and give the tender consistency that allows shredding.

## SERVING

When done, remove the roast from the heat and let sit for 15–20 minutes to allow the moisture to stabilize in the meat. (If you monitor the interior temperature, you may actually see the temperature rise as the exterior and interior temperatures level out.) Jack keeps his roast in a picnic cooler just big enough for the roast, which keeps the temperature up while the internal juices stabilize.

Cut off any excessively dry or burnt areas from the roast and discard them. Using large forks, pull the meat into shreds. Keep it warm in an aluminum tray until it is ready to serve.

Pulled pork is often mixed with a red Kansas City-style barbecue sauce, heated in a pan or slow-cooker, and served as an entrée. Sometimes it is served on a Kaiser roll with Carolina-style coleslaw on top (see recipe in the "Sides" section) and sprinkled liberally with "Pig Picking" sauce (see recipe below). But some people just like eating that smoky goodness all by itself.

## CAROLINA PIG PICKING SAUCE

1 C. cider vinegar

3 T. brown sugar

1 tsp. salt

½ tsp. black pepper

¼ tsp. red/cayenne pepper

2 T. dry mustard

Combine all ingredients and use as a sauce on pulled pork.

# Mission 3-Beef Brisket

Texas-style barbecue is usually based on beef and served with the sauce on the side, and beef brisket is the crown jewel of that part of the barbecue world. Brisket is a thick, flat cut of marbled meat with a lot of flavor that can be remarkably tender if cooked correctly.

Like pulled pork, brisket is a long cook; unlike pulled pork, it is served in slices, not shreds, so it must be cooked long enough to

make it tender but not so long that it falls apart when sliced.

Barbecued beef usually benefits from more aggressively flavored rubs, especially those featuring black pepper. I suggest the Fire and Spice Red Rub with additional black pepper. You can also vary the rub by swapping out the pepper with smoked black pepper or coarse cracked peppercorns, which are sometimes a mix of white, red, and black peppers.

## PREPARATION

Start by trimming the excess fat off the brisket so it's no thicker than ½ inch at any given spot. Pay special attention to removing most of the large v-shaped fatty layer that many briskets have on the top of the cut. Also, trim off any loose or thin pieces that might burn during the cooking process. Sprinkle the rub liberally on the meat. On this particular cut, make sure you get plenty

of rub on the sides, as they are easy to miss but constitute a significant area that needs to be sealed.

## COOKING

As with the other cuts, heat the grill to 350 degrees, add the smoker packet, and place the meat fat side up on the unheated side of the grill. Let the rub sear for about 15 minutes then reduce the temperature to 225. Check the temperature regularly, both

in the grill and in the meat. Spray a mop on the meat every 20 minutes or so. Brisket regularly takes 12–14 hours to cook, but watch the internal temperatures, as they can tell you more precisely what is going on inside. The meat is done when it reaches 180–195 degrees; while rare beef is done at 140 degrees, the higher temperature is required to make brisket tender.

When the meat is done, wrap it in foil and let it rest for 10–20 minutes then slice it and serve it hot. After slicing, brisket can be kept hot for some time in tinfoil pans in the oven if necessary. Brisket is generally served plain with the sauce on the side; often it is not served with sauce at all.

# Oh, My Gosh! The Meat Is Pink!

Sometimes inexperienced barbecue eaters get upset because the meat they are eating is partially pink inside, which makes it look raw. This may or may not be a problem. The process of smoking typically creates a pink or red "smoke ring" inside the meat. This pink does not result from undercooking but from the smoking process. Ironically, this process was used for hundreds of years to create meat that could be stored without refrigeration and still be safely eaten. I became friends with a butcher in the Lorraine section of France; he had a small brick smokehouse in his backyard, where he made the famous "Black Forest ham" for which that section of the world is famous. He told me that if he got the smoke just right, he could hang a cured ham in his window for as long as six months without it going bad.

So how do you tell if the meat is smoked or raw? A smoke ring starts from the outside and works its way in. In contrast, uncooked meat is most intensely pink at the middle and lightens toward the cooked sections.

# Mission 4—Pork Ribs

Pork ribs are the Holy Grail of barbecue and somewhat of a challenge to cook, but if you do it right, you can create a hit with your barbecue crowd every time. There are basically two kinds of ribs: the long, thin kind called St. Louis–style, or spareribs, and the shorter, thicker kind called baby backs or loin. Generally, the St. Louis–style are less expensive, but the baby backs are easier to cook, so it's a tradeoff you will have to decide on. Consider starting with St. Louis–style and then moving to baby backs; that way you will appreciate the difference.

When buying ribs, expect to purchase about ¾–1 pound per person; you can also consider 4 to 5 people per rack.

## PREPARATION

Remove the ribs from the packaging, rinse them in cold water, and pat them dry with paper towels. St. Louis–style ribs

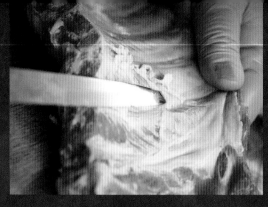

("spareribs") usually have a bone on one side of the rack and a flap of meat with no bones on the other; both should be trimmed off. These pieces make it difficult to cook and serve if they are not detached; they can be cooked directly on the grill, separate from the ribs. Cut these off and lay them aside.

On the backside of the ribs is a membrane that needs to be removed. Pull up one corner using the tip of a knife or a skewer, grab onto it using a kitchen cloth, and pull it off. Once the membrance is removed, cover the ribs with rub. This preparation can be done immediately prior to cooking or as long as 24 hours ahead. Letting the ribs sit for several hours in the fridge after you cover them with rub enables the rub to work its way deeper into the meat but is not necessary for a great result.

## COOKING

Preheat the grill to 350, and lay out the ribs on the racks so they don't touch, if

# Finishing "Off the Grill" Is Not Cheating

Sometimes the most cherished things we want to do in life have to be postponed or completed in an unorthodox fashion if we are to get them done at all! While competition cooks must use charcoal as their only heat source, the student of barbecue can use whatever tools are available to get great results.

It's common to find yourself in a situation where the outside of the meat looks great but the inside isn't done. If your ribs get a great golden look but your internal temperatures have not reached what they should, you can still get a great final product by protecting the outside surface while you finish the cooking. Some cooks wrap ribs in aluminum foil and continue cooking them on the grill, but since you can't get any more smoke flavor that way, I prefer to place the ribs in a roaster or turkey-roasting bag and finish them in a low-temperature oven. This keeps the meat from getting black while still keeping the great smoke flavor from the grill. I can monitor the temperature by pushing the thermometer probe directly through the plastic to tell when it is ready.

If you have too much to do the day of the barbecue, you can do the preliminary cooking two or three days ahead of time and then refrigerate the ribs. An hour or two before serving, finish them on the grill or in the oven. Bring them to temperature, glazing with the barbecue sauce, and enjoy the compliments.

41

# Rib Racks

While ribs can be cooked flat on the grill, I highly recommend getting a rib rack—maybe even two. Ribs are long and floppy, and the rib rack lets you cook them vertically, which takes a lot less room on your grill. I also like to cook ribs in one piece, and most racks are too short to do that, so I use two matching racks side by side so they can hold up both ends. Rib racks can be found online or at stores that sell outdoor cooking and camping supplies.

possible. If I am cooking only one side of ribs, I cut it in two and place it in one rack. If I'm cooking more, I find it is better to have two rib racks side by side to keep the ends from drooping over. Depending on your rack and the spacing, you can cook two to four sides of ribs using this method.

Once the ribs are on the rack, add smoke. After 15 minutes, lower the temperature to 225. You will need to check the ribs and spray or baste them often with your mop to avoid drying the meat. As the cooking progresses, you will notice the ends of the bones starting to stick out. They will extend ½ to ¾ inch when completely done. When the internal temperature reaches 170 degrees they should be done; after you've gained some experience, you will be able to visually gauge doneness by how far the bones stick out and how firm the meat has become. Caramelize the barbecue sauce on them, as with the chicken recipe, then cut and serve.

# Cutting Cooked Ribs

Cutting hot meat is a challenge, especially when it's covered in sizzling, sticky barbecue sauce. There are a few things that make this process easier. Besides using sterile nitrile gloves to handle the meat, I also prefer to hold the ribs vertically, bones running up and down, thin side up. Start the cut from the side where bone sticks out, then follow the curve down. If the ribs are overly tender, cut the ribs first, then lay them in a pan side by side and put the sauce on after you cut them for better presentation. Having a helper take the ribs as they're cut and arranging them really speeds up the process!

## The "Clean Bite"

When judging ribs at barbecue competition, experienced judges are looking for "the clean bite." In other words, when they bite into a rib, the meat should come off the bone cleanly and the bone should be hot. If ribs are underdone, small bits of meat will still stick to the bone. If ribs are overdone, the meat will fall off the bone when you bite into it. While you are developing your skill, it's better to err on the side of cooking too long than not long enough. Most people don't know about the clean bite, but they do know the difference between tough and tender.

# MEN USE TOOLS
## THE BARBECUE TOOLBOX

Many anthropologists believe that it is man's ability to use tools that separates him from the lower order of creatures. Whether it's a hammer, a keyboard, or a remote control, man was meant to maximize his impact on the universe by using tools. Barbecue is a manly art, because it uses tools to take a simple form of cooking (grilling) and raise it to enlightened heights (barbecue)!

If you're serious about barbecuing, you will need a collection of tools. What follows are the basics.

# The Barbecue Toolbox

- A notebook so you can record recipes and their modifications

- Good tongs (capable of picking up large cuts of meat)

- A smoker box or tinfoil for smoker packets

- Wood chips (start with hickory)

- Meat thermometer

- Spray bottle for mops (or a little mop if you use thicker mop sauces)

- Spray bottle for water (for fire control and cleaning)

- Rib rack (or two, based on how many sides of ribs you cook)

- Shaker bottles for rub

- Disposable nitrile gloves for slathering and cutting meat

- Barbecue brush (I have found the silicone variety work well and don't shred )

- Aluminum foil and pans (for warming, carrying, and serving meats)

# Cleaning the Grill

While most "professional" smokers may have thick black coatings on them from years of smoke, your grill itself should be cleaned from time to time so you don't get unappetizing black marks on lighter-colored meats. A friend from New York showed me a clever way of cleaning that I had never seen before. Cooks in the Empire State do it this way: Heat the grill to over 400 degrees and then spray the grill itself with water from a spray bottle. The water explodes upon contact and takes a lot of the grease and debris with it. The high temperature also carbonizes the residue, much like a self-cleaning oven. Between those two processes, I find there is very little left to clean off with my steel brush—and a long, tedious job becomes quick and painless.

# SIDE DISHES

Life was not meant to be lived alone; meaningful living is achieved when we have good relationships with our spouse and friends. In much the same way, great barbecue is more meaningful and enjoyable when served with the right side dishes.

As in relationships, there are many different types of flavors. Some sides, such as baked beans, are savory and similar to the barbecued meat itself. Others, like coleslaw or potato salad, are lighter and meant to contrast and compliment. Traditionally, there are several basic sides that seem to be served universally at barbecues around the country, but this is by no means comprehensive. As in life, you will find the companion sides that work for you; some will never change, while others will come and go.

# Barbecue Beans

Barbecue beans are one of the mainstays of barbecue sides and are as varied as the cooks who make them. Some attribute their origins to the French Canadian lumberjacks who made their version of baked beans, called cassoulet, sweetened with maple syrup and cooked in great earthenware containers that simmered in buried fire pits while they worked in the forests. Beans from the eastern and southern regions of the United States tend to be sweet, and cooks who make them often start with pork and beans as their base. Western varieties tend to be savory, spicy, and based on larger beans, such as kidney beans.

While most barbecue cooks use their leftover meat and rub to flavor their beans, I prefer to use a completely different seasoning so they will stand out from the meat itself. There are many recipes that start with dried

# Heating and Serving Baked Beans

Beans are one of the most popular side dishes at our barbecues, so we make large amounts and we make them early. There's just one problem with that: beans burn easily, and it's hard to keep them at temperature or to reheat them without burning them. Our solution? When we make beans early, we keep them hot in a large slow-cooker during the day until they are needed. If they need to be reheated in small amounts, the microwave works well; make sure to cover them while heating, as some beans explode from microwave radiation. The easiest and most traditional method is to heat them in the oven in a bean pot. They won't burn that way—and, besides, that's probably the reason they're known as baked beans in the first place.

# Cooking Too Fast

A man I admire greatly who used to be a fighter pilot in Europe told a story about flying in turbulence. As a pilot, he was always trying to get to his destination as fast as possible—except when turbulence hit. I would have thought that the best thing to do in that situation would be to increase the power and speed and get through it as fast as possible, but he said the number-one rule was to slow down then figure out if a change of course or altitude would help avoid the storm or if you were just going to have to plow through. It's like driving over speed bumps—if you go too fast, you're planted on the roof of your car. If you take them slow, they don't affect you much at all. We live in a stormy world. When we cook too fast and things look like they're going to burn up, slow down until you figure out what's best to do next!

beans, but pork and beans are also popular. The following is a basic recipe based on pork and beans that was given to me by my Aunt Dora at a family funeral in Canada.

## AUNT DORA'S FUNERAL BEANS

1 lb. hamburger

4 T. chili powder

Salt and pepper to taste

2 medium onions, diced finely

2 53-oz. cans of pork and beans

1 C. ketchup

¾ C. brown sugar

Hot sauce to taste

Break up the hamburger and fry in a large frying pan. When it starts to brown, sprinkle with chili powder, salt, and pepper; stir until mixed. Add onion and continue cooking until onion is translucent. Remove pork cubes from pork and beans and drain off any excess sauce from the can. Add remaining ingredients. Serve after the mixture is well heated.

# FROM SCRATCH VOYAGEUR BAKED BEANS

Here is a baked bean recipe made from scratch, dedicated to those early French Canadian explorers. While there is a method of soaking and cooking dried beans, it can be unpredictable in terms of cooking times, and I prefer the ease of the slow-cooker method, as used in this recipe.

5 C. dried Navy or Great Northern beans (approximate), cooked, or 50 oz. canned beans

5–6 slices bacon

1 large onion, cut finely

1 C. ketchup

3 T. molasses

2 T. yellow mustard

2 T. Worcestershire sauce

Ground red pepper to taste

½ C. maple syrup (optional)

The night or early morning before needed, place the dried beans in a slow-cooker and cover with water. Do not add salt. Cook beans until tender (about 8–10 hours; if you are using a Crock Pot brand slow-cooker, cook on High). Set aside. Cut bacon into bits and cook until crispy. Add finely diced onion to the bacon and cook until the onion is translucent. Pour beans into a baking dish; add bacon/onions and remaining ingredients. Stir well to combine. Bake at 350 degrees for 45 minutes, or until mixture bubbles evenly around the edges.

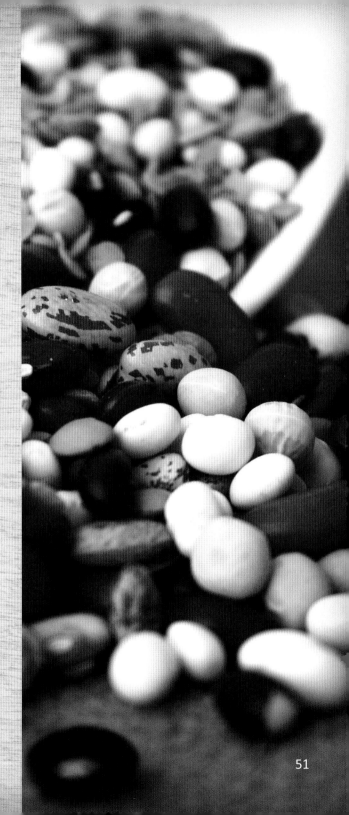

# Coleslaw

If coleslaw is not the second most popular barbecue side dish, it is at least within striking distance. Made from grated cabbage and a wide range of additional ingredients, coleslaw seems to have no limits in terms of types and variations. Sometimes sweet, sometimes tangy, or sometimes fruity, coleslaw varies widely across the country. Here are two contrasting recipes to try.

## INTERMOUNTAIN CREAMY COLESLAW

This is an example of the sweet and creamy flavor that seems to be preferred in the Intermountain West. Use this recipe if you find someone who says they don't like coleslaw. It is "knee-bucklingly good."

## DRESSING

1 C. mayonnaise/Miracle Whip (or ½ C. of each)

½ C. sugar

3 T. vinegar

2 T. mustard

¼ tsp. salt

¼ tsp. pepper

Mix all ingredients together to create a dressing. Mix with shredded cabbage just until the cabbage is lightly covered. When cabbage is mixed with the dressing, moisture in the cabbage will be drawn out, so it's important to not add too much dressing. Some cooks add a couple of teaspoons of salt to the cabbage shreds and let them sit overnight; before making the salad, they drain the excess moisture. If it all possible, make the salad the day before and let the flavors blossom overnight. Coleslaw, like friendship, gets better with age.

# FIRE AND SPICE CAROLINA COLESLAW DRESSING

This Carolina-style dressing is heavy with the tang of vinegar and the spice of pepper and celery seed. This salad is traditionally served as a contrasting flavor on top of mounds of sweet, mouth-watering pulled pork, sprinkled with pig picking sauce, and served on a Kaiser bun.

2 C. white vinegar

¾ C. sugar

2 T. salt

2 tsp. black pepper

2 T. celery seed

Mix all ingredients and refrigerate until it's time to dress and serve the coleslaw. If possible, mix ingredients 24 hours prior to use to allow the flavors to blossom.

## VARIATIONS AND MIX-INS

While coleslaw is traditionally made from shredded cabbage, it tends to look very pale if that is the only ingredient. If you want to make a great presentation, add purple cabbage and matchstick carrots to make it darker, more colorful, and more appealing. In the West it is also popular to include "mix-ins." Try adding some of the following: ½ C. crushed pineapple, ½ C. thinly sliced apples, ¼ C. chopped almonds or walnuts, ⅓ C. raisins, or ⅓ C. dried cranberries. Use whatever sounds appealing! Any of these can be used to add interesting flavor and texture. If you use pineapple or apples, you may wish to cut back on or cut out the sugar—again, that depends on *your* tastes.

# Potato Salad

One of the biggest dilemmas I have when serving barbecue is whether to serve it with coleslaw or potato salad. Coleslaw creates a fresh, crispy contrast to the meat, but potato salad is the ultimate companion for baked beans of any kind. My wife, Susan, developed this recipe for potato salad that has an additional tang from dill weed—a spice she uses generously.

## SUSAN'S DILLY POTATO SALAD

3 lbs. potatoes, peeled and boiled

6 eggs, boiled

½ C. onion, finely chopped (1 medium onion)

1 C. celery, finely chopped

2 T. dill weed, to taste

2 T. mustard

1 C. mayonnaise

1 C. Miracle Whip

¾ C. dill pickles, diced

Garlic salt, to taste

Black pepper, to taste

Potato salad is best when made a day ahead of time so everything can chill and the flavors can blossom. Cut the cooled potatoes and eggs in cubes; add the onion, celery, dill, and mustard. In a small bowl, combine the mayonnaise and Miracle Whip; gradually add mixed dressing to the potato mixture until it reaches the desired consistency. Add the rest of the ingredients and stir to combine.

# Mashed Potatoes

Mashed potatoes are a relative newcomer to the barbecue world as a side dish but they have quickly become a standard, as they extend the flavors of the barbecued meats and sauces and make the meat go further. This recipe for garlic mashed potatoes can stand alone or be served with gravy with other entrees. I prefer Yukon Gold potatoes for their thin skin and ease of mashing. Mashed potatoes can be kept warm in a slow-cooker or an aluminum foil pan in the oven for several hours to free up time to do other things just before serving.

## GARLIC MASHED POTATOES

5 lbs. potatoes

8 oz. cream cheese

8 oz. sour cream

½ C. butter (1 stick)

1 T. garlic powder

Boil the potatoes about 20 minutes, until tender. Drain off the water but reserve some for mashing. Let the potatoes sit out of the water for 5–10 minutes to let the carbs blossom, then mash in the remaining ingredients. Use the leftover potato water to thin the mashed potatoes to the right consistency. These potatoes are great with anything that has barbecue sauce on it!

# Funeral Potatoes

Here in the Intermountain West, funeral potatoes rank very high on the comfort food menu. This is a type of au gratin potato dish that is consistently prepared by women's service groups to feed families at luncheons that immediately follow funerals. They gained popularity because they are easy to fix in large amounts and are simply delicious! In this recipe, we use pepper jack cheese instead of the regular cheddar, but we have also tried other variations—so experiment based on your taste and what's in the pantry. We've listed alternates for most of the ingredients in this recipe. These are wonderful with Aunt Dora's Funeral Beans, especially during the cooler temperatures of spring or autumn.

32- to 48-oz. pkg. frozen hash brown cubes, thawed (you can also use potato shreds or fresh potatoes)

2 10-oz. cans cream of chicken soup (or cream of celery or cream of mushroom)

2 C. shredded pepper jack cheese (you can also use cheddar, gruyere, or add ¼ C. Parmesan to any cheese)

1 C. sour cream (or 8 oz. cream cheese)

¾ C. minced onion (or minced green onion)

½ C. (1 stick) butter

Topping (optional):

1 C. crushed corn flakes (or crushed corn chips)

½ C. shredded cheese (optional)

In a large bowl, mix all but the topping ingredients. Spray a 9 x 13 glass baking dish with nonstick cooking spray and pour in the potato mixture. Cover and bake at 350 degrees for 40 minutes (you will need to cook it longer if you use fresh potatoes). If you want to use the topping, uncover the potatoes and sprinkle with corn flakes and/or cheese; bake an additional 5 minutes.

# THE NEXT STEP– OTHER TECHNIQUES

In barbecue, everyone generally chooses his own techniques to get the results he wants. Now that you have been introduced to the basics of barbecue, here are some additional techniques to experiment with that will give your cooking a uniqueness that will be all your own.

# Brining

Brining is a surprisingly simple process of soaking your meat in a mixture of water and salt. It is used for meat that tends to dry during cooking, such as chicken breast, turkey, and fish. While some brines may have other ingredients for flavoring mixed in, the following basic brine recipe is a good place to start.

## BASIC BRINE

¼ C. non-iodized kosher or pretzel salt

1 pint hot water

3 pints cold water

Dissolve the salt in the hot water. Stir in the cold water.

Wash meat thoroughly; place it in a deep container and cover it completely with brine. Soak for as long as 2 hours. Soaking too long can cause the meat to become rubbery. A simple rule of thumb is to add the same amount of sugar as salt to any recipe in which you have soaked the meat in brine.

# Marinating

Marinating is similar to brining because it involves soaking the meat, but the marinade mixture will feature a tenderizing agent as well as flavorings. Ingredients such as vinegar, lemon juice, pineapple juice, lime juice, mango juice, and many others help break down the components of the meat that make it tough. Be sure not to overmarinate, as meat can become mushy if too much is used or it is soaked too long. Following are two basic marinades to try; the procedure is the same for both.

## CHILI LIME TENDERLOIN MARINADE FOR PORK AND CHICKEN

- 1 12-oz. can limeade drink concentrate
- 1 C. water
- 2 T. habañero hot sauce
- 2 T. salt

## GARLIC MARINADE FOR BEEF

- 1 C. water
- ½ C. balsamic vinegar
- ½ C. lemon juice
- ¼ C. vegetable oil
- ¼ C. soy sauce
- ¼ C. brown sugar
- 3 T. Worcestershire sauce
- 3 T. minced garlic
- 2 T. salt
- 2 T. black pepper

## PROCEDURE

Mix ingredients thoroughly. Place meat in a gallon-size reclosable bag; pour marinade into the bag. Release as much air as possible so the marinade completely covers the meat, and then seal the bag. Place the bag in a glass baking dish in the fridge for 2–4 hours. Discard marinade after use.

# MANTI CHICKEN MARINADE

Thousands of people flock to Manti, Utah, every summer to see the local outdoor summer pageant—and as part of the experience, grills fire up all across town to cook up this delightful local specialty. The poultry farms in the area provide fresh turkey breast for the event, but the recipe works just as well with chicken. While not everyone makes it to Manti, this dish has a following across the United States. This version makes enough for about 5 pounds of chicken or turkey breast.

24 oz. lemon-lime soda

1 C. vegetable oil

1 C. soy sauce

1 T. ground horseradish

1 tsp. garlic salt

Mix ingredients. Marinate the meat overnight in reclosable plastic bags, non-reactive glass, or covered plastic containers. This is one recipe where I don't recommend a rub.

# Injecting

Injecting uses the same principles as marinating and brining, but it is used in dense meats such as pork tenderloin and large turkeys that are difficult to cover with brines and marinades. The procedure uses a large injection needle designed for the purpose. These culinary syringes can be purchased at most stores that carry cooking supplies. Like a marinade, an injection is usually a mixture of salt, flavorings, and tenderizing agents thin enough to pass through the needle and be injected directly into the meat. The following basic recipes work equally well in turkey and pork. The procedure is the same for both.

## APPLE INJECTION

3 C. apple juice

1 C. sugar

⅓ C. salt

2 T. Worcestershire sauce

## FRUITY TURKEY INJECTION

12 oz. apple juice concentrate

12 oz. orange juice concentrate

1 C. hot water

¼ C. salt

## PROCEDURE

Mix all ingredients until salt and sugars are completely dissolved. Place the tip of the needle in the mixture and pull back the plunger to fill the syringe. Insert the needle deep into the meat and inject the marinade while slowly pulling the needle out. Repeat this process every couple of inches across the meat and in different directions. Don't worry if some of the mixture leaks out of the meat; that's normal.

# Slathering

Slathering is a traditional form of prepping meat by covering the cut of meat with yellow mustard and rubbing it in by hand. This is another recipe where I recommend wearing protective gloves. Mustard slathers provide some tenderizing from the vinegar and a slight addition of flavor from the mustard. They are often used to help rubs stick to the meat better. There are a lot of different mustards that can be used, but plain yellow seems to be the most popular. Sometimes other ingredients are added to make it interesting. I like the combination in this recipe.

## FIRE AND SPICE MUSTARD MIX SLATHER

½ C. yellow mustard

½ C. spicy brown mustard

¼ C. brown sugar

1 T. Worcestershire sauce

½ tsp. red pepper

In a small bowl, mix all ingredients until the sugar is dissolved. Rub liberally over meat prior to cooking.

# Mops

As mentioned earlier, *mops* are thin liquids applied to the meat during cooking to keep them from drying out; they also add flavor. In Southern-style barbecue they are often made with vinegar and peppers. Personally, I prefer simple mops like apple juice that can be applied through the nozzle of a spray bottle (this requires apple juice from concentrates or apple juice that has been filtered so it doesn't clog the bottle). The traditional method, however, is to apply mops with a small mop like the ones once used for washing dishes. (Yes, I know it sounds crazy—you apply a mop with a mop!) Whichever method you use, wait long enough after you start cooking the meat to give the rub enough time to set. If you don't, you may wash it off.

Mops are optional for short cooks like chicken and sausage, but indispensable for long cooks like ribs and pulled pork. There are a lot of spiced mop recipes, but keep in mind that they will add to the flavors of your rub and will need to be used judiciously.

Here's my favorite mop recipe.

## FIRE AND SPICE "JUST MOPPIN' UP" SAUCE

2 C. vinegar

½ C. sugar

½ C. vegetable oil

½ C. lemon juice

½ tsp. cayenne

2 T. salt

2 T. pepper

In a small, deep bowl, mix all ingredients. Mop onto cooking meat as necessary to keep moist.

# The Power of Attentiveness

Many barbecue projects take a long time to complete and give you a lot of time to sit and visit or just enjoy the day with a cold glass of something. It's important to remember, however, that when it's time to do something, it needs to be done—especially when it comes to mops. One day I was cooking several large pork roasts that were going to take about fourteen hours to cook. I had other commitments and couldn't be there to watch them and make sure everything was okay. My teenage daughter was eager to help and told me she would watch the roasts and put the mop on regularly. I had been spraying them with apple juice, and although I accepted her offer, I worried that she would not be as attentive as I would be. So instead of having her spray them down every twenty to thirty minutes, I told her they had to be sprayed every fifteen to twenty minutes, thinking she would forget and we would get about the right timing.

As the day progressed I called home and asked her if the roasts had turned dark brown or black yet, as pulled pork often does. She said they had not. I had her check the temperature in the grill, thinking it might be out of propane. It was perfect. Late in the afternoon I was getting very nervous; her description of the meat still did not sound right. I rushed home as soon as I could and discovered she had kept to the spraying schedule *exactly* as I had asked her to—and instead of the meat looking like a meteor, it had a golden brown crust of apple sugar from the juice on the outside. It was one of the most beautiful sights I have ever seen and was a real hit at the office party that night.

Good relationships are like good barbecue; they may not require all of our time, but if we spend small amounts regularly, the results can be well worth the effort.

# WHERE TO FROM HERE?

Now that you have learned the fundamental foundations of barbecue, you have the basic tools to start on the path to personal barbecue greatness!

## Some of the Great American Barbecue Regions

1. Memphis—Known for pulled pork shoulder with tomato-based barbecue sauce.

2. The Carolinas—Known for their vinegary pig picking and mustard-based sauces.

3. Kansas City—Known for pork ribs smoked with a dry rub.

4. Texas—Known for beef barbecue,

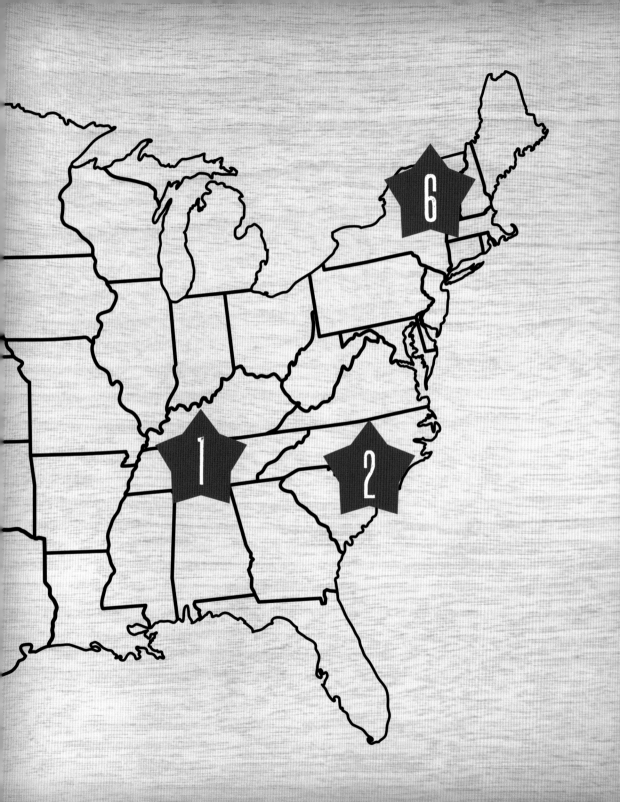

particularly brisket.

5. Utah/Idaho Intermountain—Known for Manti Chicken and Funeral Potatoes.

6. New England and Quebec—Known for baked beans.

7. California—Known for tri-tip beef barbecue.

8. Alaska—Known for its amazing smoked salmon.

9. **YOUR BACKYARD**—known for good food, good friends, and your secret family barbecue recipes!

# NOTES AND SECRET RECIPES